BIBLE
101
SIX SESSIONS FOR SM

CW00996376

FOUNDATIONS

How we got our Bible

WILLOW CREEK
RESOURCES

BiLL DONaHUe
BILL DONAHUE, SERIES EDITOR

≈
ivp

InterVarsity Press
Downers Grove, Illinois
Leicester, England

InterVarsity Press
P.O. Box 1400, Downers Grove, IL 60515, USA
World Wide Web: www.ivpress.com
E-mail: mail@ivpress.com

Inter-Varsity Press, England
38 De Montfort Street, Leicester LE1 7GP, England

InterVarsity Press®, U.S.A., is the book-publishing division of InterVarsity Christian Fellowship/USA®, a
student movement active on campus at hundreds of universities, colleges and schools of nursing in the
United States of America, and a member movement of the International Fellowship of Evangelical Students.
For information about local and regional activities, write Public Relations Dept., InterVarsity Christian
Fellowship/USA, 6400 Schroeder Rd., P.O. Box 7895, Madison, WI 53707-7895.

Inter-Varsity Press, England, is the book-publishing division of the Universities and Colleges Christian
Fellowship (formerly the Inter-Varsity Fellowship), a student movement linking Christian Unions in
universities and colleges throughout the United Kingdom and the Republic of Ireland, and a member
movement of the International Fellowship of Evangelical Students. For information about local and
national activities write to UCCF, 38 De Montfort Street, Leicester LE1 7GP.

Cover design: Grey Matter Group

Photo image: Michael VanderKallen

Chapter icons: Roberta Polfus

USA ISBN 0-8308-2061-2

UK ISBN 0-85111-527-6

Printed in the United States of America ∞

19	18	17	16	15	14	13	12	11	10	9	8	7	6	5	4	3	2	1
15	14	13	12	11	10	09	08	07	06	05	04	03	02	01	00			

Contents

Introduction

Some time ago, Russ Robinson (director of small group ministries at Willow Creek Community Church and concept editor on these guides) and I were talking about how to help groups get a firm grip on the Word of God. Both of us had studied and taught courses on the Bible, but what about small groups? What if we could put something together that could be studied as a group and yet have much of the information people would normally find in a class or course? Well, hats off to Russ, who came up with the idea for Bible 101 and cast the vision for what it could look like. Soon we were outlining the books and the result is what you have before you. So welcome to the Bible 101 adventure, a place where truth meets life!

Traditionally the subject matter in this series has been reserved for classroom teaching or personal study. Both are places where this curriculum could be used. But this work is primarily targeted at small groups, places where men and women, old and young, rich and poor gather together in community to engage fully with the truth of God's Word. These little communities can be transforming in ways that classrooms and personal study cannot.

Few things in life are more fulfilling than drawing out the deep truths of Scripture and then seeing them at work to change a life into the image of Christ. Getting a firm grip on the Bible and its teachings is paramount to a mature and intelligent walk with God. We are to worship him with all our heart, soul, mind and strength. And the Word of God is central to accomplishing God's desire that we be fully devoted to him.

The team from Willow Creek—staff and volunteers alike—has labored diligently to provide you with a group-friendly process for understanding the Bible. Kathy Dice, Gerry Mathisen, Judson Poling, Michael Redding and I have worked to provide something that merges content and process, learning and application. Now it is up to you to work together to discover the riches that lie ahead for those willing to do some work and take a few risks. But we know you are more than ready for that challenge!

To make these studies more productive, here are a few suggestions and guidelines to help you along the way. Read carefully so that you get the most out of this series.

Purpose

This series is designed to ground a Christ-follower in the study and understanding of Scripture. It is not designed for someone who became a Christian last week, though sections of it would certainly be good. And it is not as rigorous as a Bible college class or seminary course might be. Bible 101 means *foundational,* but not easy or light. So be prepared for some challenge and some stretching. This may be the first time you are exposed to certain theological concepts or terms, or to some more in-depth methods of Bible study. Celebrate the challenge and strive to do your best. Peter tells us to "make every effort" to add knowledge to our faith. It will take some effort, but I can guarantee it will be well worth it!

Prayer

When approaching the Word of God, you will need to keep a submissive and teachable attitude. The Holy Spirit is eager to teach you, but you must be willing to receive knowledge, encouragement, correction and challenge. One educator has taught that all learning is the result of failed expectations. We hope that in some ways you are ambushed by the truth and stumble upon new and unfamiliar territory that startles you into new ways of thinking about God and relating to him through Christ.

Practice

Each session has the same format, except (in some cases) the last session. For five meetings you will learn skills, discuss material and readings, work together as a team, and discover God's truths in fresh and meaningful ways. The sixth session will be an opportunity to put all you have learned into practice. Studies are designed as follows.

 Establishing Base Camp (5-10 minutes). A question or icebreaker to focus the meeting.

Mapping the Trail (5-10 minutes). An overview of where we are headed.

 Beginning the Ascent (30 minutes). The main portion of the discussion time.

Gaining a Foothold (3 minutes). Information to read that identifies core issues and ideas to keep you on track with the journey.

 Trailmarkers (10 minutes). Important Scriptures or discussions for memorization or reflection.

 Teamwork (15 minutes). A group activity (sometimes done in subgroups) to build community and share understanding of what was learned.

 Reaching the Summit (5 minutes). A chance to summarize and look back at what has been learned or accomplished.

Close in Prayer (as long as you want!). An opportunity to pray for one another and ask God to deepen the truths of Scripture in you.

You can take some shortcuts or take longer as the group decides, but strive to stay on schedule for a 75- to 90-minute meeting, including prayer time. You will also want to save time to attend to personal needs. This will vary by group and can also be accomplished in personal relationships you develop between meetings.

Preparation

Preparation? There is none! Well, almost none. For some sessions reading ahead will be suggested to provide an overview. But the sessions are designed to be worked through together. We find this builds a sense of team and community, and is also more fun! And there is something about "discovery in the moment" rather than merely discussing what everyone has already discovered outside the meeting that provides a sense of adventure.

We wish you the best as you draw truth from the Word of God for personal transformation, group growth and kingdom impact!

Bill Donahue, Series Editor
Vice President, Small Group Ministries
Willow Creek Association

Session 1

How We Got Our Bible
Revelation & Inspiration
Discovering how God speaks to us.

 ### Establishing Base Camp

On our tenth anniversary my wife and I went on a guided, private horseback ride through several hundred acres of beautiful Wisconsin countryside. Rolling hills, farmland, heavily wooded forests and plush clearings marked the fertile landscape. Most of the time we had little idea where we were or where we were going. But our guide was intimately acquainted with the landscape, the personalities of the horses and the intended destination. He was also aware of our limited riding experience. Without him our journey would have been a haphazard collection of miscalculations, guesses and mistakes.

If we hadn't had a guide, my hunch is that we'd still be somewhere in the backwoods of the Midwest trying to navigate by the stars. "Isn't that the big dipper?" I'd ask my wife. She, being a godly and loving woman, would be thinking to herself, *Actually, I think I married the big dipper.* Ah yes, another anniversary etched in two lovers' memories. . . . So I'm glad we had a guide—someone to mark the way, lead us onward and keep us from error. We still did the riding, used our own style, added our creativity to the trip and even chose our own horses. But it was clear who was leading the way.

✓ Describe a time when someone, a guide perhaps, led you into unknown territory or through a new experience. What in particular did the guide do? Not do? Why did you feel you could trust the guide?

Mapping the Trail

✓ If you were to ask (or have asked) people where they think the Bible came from, what responses would you expect?

✓ Why do you think there is such widespread misunderstanding?

✓ What do you understand about the origin of the Bible?

Beginning the Ascent

Briefly review the chart below and then discuss the definitions and significance of each of the terms listed. (Review the entire chart, but focus on the concepts of "Revelation" and "Inspiration." In session two we will cover "Manuscripts" and "Translations.")

The Flow of Revelation

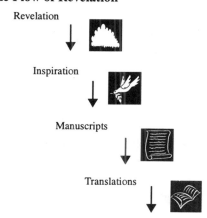

Revelation

Inspiration

Manuscripts

Translations

Key Terms

Revelation: God's self-disclosure. God reveals himself to us in two key ways—general revelation and special revelation.

General Revelation: God shows us who he is and how he works through events, in creation and in our hearts (Acts 17:24-31; Psalm 19:1-6; Romans 1:18-23).

Special Revelation: These are unique, specific ways in which God makes himself and his acts known. They include Scripture (the primary way God speaks to us, 2 Timothy 3:16-17), visions (Acts 16:6-10), dreams (Matthew 2:13), the guidance of the Holy Spirit (Acts 20:22-23) and listening prayer (Acts 13:1-3).

Inspiration: This is the process by which God guided the writers of Scripture so that they wrote the words he wanted written. Inspiration means "God-breathed." The source of the Scriptures is God. When he inspired the writers, he guided the process and guarded the content through the work of the Holy Spirit (2 Timothy 3:16-17; 2 Peter 1:20-21).

Manuscripts: The original documents that comprise the Scriptures were copied primarily on parchment or papyrus. Then copies were made so that people could have access to them. This took a long time and was done with painstaking care to ensure that accuracy was maintained.

Translation: The process whereby original language manuscripts were copied into the language of a certain people or culture. Once in that language, various versions may result (in English, for example, the King James Version, New International Version and New Revised Standard Version). Copies of manuscripts were translated through the years to provide us with the Bible we have today.

The Scriptures are the result of a process guided and protected from error by God. The "Flow of Reve-

DUAL AUTHORSHIP OF SCRIPTURE
When we took our trail ride, our guide protected us from error and led us along the way. In the same way, the Holy Spirit guided and guarded the writers of Scripture so that they wrote the words of God without error. Writers used their own personal style and methods, but always under the watchful influence of the Holy Spirit. According to 2 Peter 1:20-21: "Above all, you must understand that no prophecy of Scripture came about by the prophet's own interpretation. For prophecy never had its origin in the will of man, but men spoke from God as they were carried along by the Holy Spirit."

lation" chart shows this process. God revealed himself and his deeds to people (revelation). Under his guidance certain men wrote his words and story so that we could all know God's truth (inspiration). The words were recorded and became the original writings of the Bible (manuscripts). Then over time these manuscripts were copied and translated into various languages so that all men and women could read God's truth for themselves (translations).

Gaining a Foothold

God revealed himself to people in words, appearances, events and in their hearts. He took the first steps in making himself known to us. Then, to ensure that his truth was recorded for all generations to know his amazing grace and love, he chose writers to tell his story. To be certain that the story was accurate and complete, God's Spirit guided the process and guarded the content. The final product is an accurate, truthful and authoritative document we call *The Holy Bible*. Over the years it has been translated into many languages and versions. What we have today, in English, is the Word of God. We can test what we believe God is saying to us against the written truth of the Scriptures, the final authority for how we live the Christian life.

Trailmarkers

Read 2 Timothy 3:16-17 and 2 Peter 1:20-21.

✓ What do these passages say about the Scriptures?

✓ What do they say about God's work and the writers' work?

Teamwork

On a flight from Toronto to Chicago, I sat next to a young woman who had just graduated college a few years ago. She was pursuing an advance degree in accounting and was quite intelligent. After we talked for awhile, I told her I was coming from a conference where I was training some church leaders. We eventually started talking about spiritual matters, including questions about the Bible. She asked me: "Is the New Testament a different Bible from the Old Testament? I always wondered how the Bible was written. Can you tell me?"

✓ In the space provided (and without looking at your notes) answer her question. Write a clear and concise description of how we got our Bible in a way that she would understand. Then select a partner and trade descriptions. Using your study guide and notes, give each other feedback on the accuracy and clarity of the description.

Reaching the Summit

Briefly review the definitions of *inspiration, revelation, manuscript* and *translation* by stating them in your own words. Spend time in prayer thanking God for his word and the truth of his revelation to us.

Revelation:

Inspiration:

Manuscript:

Translation:

Next Session

Look at various versions of the Bible to get a sense for how they are translated. Try the King James Version, New King James, New International Verson, New American Standard, New Living Translation, the Living Bible, The Message or the New Revised Standard version. What do you notice about how they are written? You might want to bring a second version of your choice to the meeting next time. Also, you might want to briefly look at the material for next session. Though it will be covered in the meeting, it has more information than most studies in this series.

Close in Prayer

Focus on praying for people you know who do not believe or understand the Bible, asking God to provide opportunities to speak with them after you have increased your confidence in the Word through this study.

Session 2

How We Got Our Bible
Manuscripts & Translations

How the Bible came to us through manuscripts and translations.

Establishing Base Camp

One summer I worked with a team to plant a church in Austria. We worked closely with churches and Christian students in Graz, in the southeastern part of the country, trying to generate interest in the gospel and build relationships with the people. At the end of the summer the nationals would continue the work.

I speak some German, so it was fun to get to know the language better and use it every day. Sometimes, however, people wanted to practice their English with us. I remember talking with a man who was eager to use his English. He was describing some shopping he was going to do and then made this statement: "I want to become a pair of shoes!" We had to hold back our laughter, partly because I knew how many times I had butchered my German while trying to communicate with locals. But it was a funny statement.

In German the word *bekommen* means "to receive" but sounds just like the English word *become*. He had made a humorous error, and instead of translating the word, he had transliterated it. He wanted to receive (or have) a new pair of shoes, not become one!

Transliteration is actually one way to translate a word from one language to another. For example, in the Bible we have the word *baptize*. In Greek it is *baptizo* and was often used to describe dipping a fabric into dye to change the color. We did not have an English equivalent for the word, so when scholars translated the text, they simply transliterated the word (turning its Greek sound into an English word—*baptize*).

✓ Describe a time when someone "mistranslated" something

you wrote or said. How did this affect the content of what was being communicated? Did it cause any problems?

 ## Mapping the Trail

John 1:18 is a powerful verse in the Bible, stating that Jesus has come to show us who God is and to make God known to us. Observe how various English versions translate the verse. As you look at them, discuss the differences and the impact they have on the meaning.

King James Version (KJV): "No man hath seen God at any time; the only begotten Son, which is in the bosom of the Father, He hath declared Him."

New Revised Standard Version (NRSV): "No one has ever seen God. It is God the only Son, who is close to the Father's heart, who has made him known."

New American Standard Bible (NASB): "No man has seen God at any time; the only begotten God, who is in the bosom of the Father, He has explained *Him*."

New International Version (NIV): "No one has ever seen God, but God the One and Only, who is at the Father's side, has made him known."

Note: both the NIV and NASB have footnotes to this verse, stating that manuscripts dated later have "only begotten Son" instead of "God." It is the earliest manuscripts in our possession that say "God."

New Living Translation (NLT): "No one has ever seen God. But his only Son, who is himself God, is near to the Father's heart; he has told us about him."

Living Bible (TLB): "No one has ever actually seen God, but, of course, His only Son has, for He is the companion of the Father and has told us all about Him."

Amplified New Testament (AMP): "No man has ever seen God at any time; the only unique Son, the only-begotten God, Who is in the bosom [that is, the intimate presence] of the Father, He has declared Him—He has revealed Him, brought Him out where He can be seen; He has interpreted Him, and He has made Him known."

The Message: "No one has ever seen God, not so much as a glimpse. This one-of-a-kind-God-Son-Word, who exists at the very heart of the Father, has made him plain as day."

Observations:

Beginning the Ascent

First review together the definitions for revelation and inspiration on the chart on page 10. Though we are focusing on the manuscripts and translations, we want to keep the bigger picture in mind.

Now read the definitions and comments for manuscripts and translations on page 10 and below, taking note that we have added additional information to the brief definition from last session.

Manuscripts: The original documents that comprise the Scriptures, copied primarily on parchment or papyrus.

The process: Once the originals were written, copies were made by scribes and monks so that more people could have access to them. This took a long time and was done with painstaking care to ensure that accuracy was maintained. The material used for writing lasted only twenty to forty years, depending on the climate and quality of parchment, so copyists had to keep making new manuscripts to preserve the text from being destroyed.

Fact: According to Norman Geisler, writing in *Christian Apologetics,* there are over 5,000 Greek manuscripts containing all or part of the New Testament. Compare this to manuscripts concerning Julius Caesar's life (10) and histories of ancient Greece and Rome (no more than 200 copies from various authors). Even the *Iliad,* written by Homer in the ninth century B.C., has only 643 copies.

Fact: Until moveable-type printing was invented in 1455, all copies of the Bible were made by hand. The Jewish scribes valued the sacred Old Testament text so much that they numbered certain Hebrew letters on every page that they copied. The middle letter of the manuscript was marked. So, if while making a copy, the letters did not line up with the original, they assumed there was an error in copying and destroyed the entire page and began over again.

If we trust the sources used for our history classes in universities, why not trust the Scripture? It has far more accuracy and evidence for quality. I doubt the writers of Caesar's time, and those who made copies of those writings, took such care. The biblical translations we hold are based on manuscripts of the highest quality and accuracy of all ancient literature combined!

Translation process: Translators of the Bible must decide to hold two things in tension: accuracy with respect to the original words, and clarity for the reader in the receptor language (the language of the reader). Not all figures of speech, idioms or concepts translate across language barriers, so choices must be made. How do you remain true to the text but communicate the truth of that text in phrases and words familiar to the culture you are writing to?

> Consider Tacitus, the Roman historian who wrote his *Annals of Imperial Rome* in about A.D. 116. His first six books exist today in only one manuscript, and it was copied about A.D. 850. Books eleven through sixteen are in another manuscript dating from the eleventh century. Books seven through ten are lost. Thus, there is a long gap between the time that Tacitus sought his information and wrote it down and the only existing copies. The quantity of New Testament material is almost embarrassing compared with other works of antiquity. (Bruce Metzger, as quoted in *The Case for Christ* by Lee Strobel.)

Translation: The process by which original language manuscripts were copied into the language of a certain people or culture. Once in that language, various versions may result (in English, for example, the King James Version, New International Version and New Revised Standard Version). Copies of manuscripts were translated through the years to provide us with the Bible we have today.

Here is the general theory of translation.

Translations and Versions

A *translation* is a work created from the original languages (like the KJV, NIV or NLT). Some translations are also versions.

A *version* can be a revision of an English translation (like the NASB, which was a revision of the earlier American Standard Version, based on the KJV). Hebrew and Greek sources are consulted, but a version does not necessarily translate directly from the original Hebrew, Aramaic and Greek texts.

Translation Methods

A *literal translation* means striving to stay as close as possible to the original wording, even if some of the meaning or understanding is lost (NASB, NRSV, KJV).

A *paraphrase* (like the Living Bible or The Message) adds interpretive comments within the text. It is not an accurate word-for-word reflection of the original but tries to convey the meaning of the text even if new words have to be added in order to ensure that the meaning is understood.

A *dynamic equivalent translation* lies between a literal translation and a paraphrase, staying close to the original text but translating idioms and figures of speech unique to the biblical languages into equivalent idioms and figures of speech in the new language.

Compare the various versions of Ezekiel 21:12 that follow.

> "It is quite easy to prove that our Bible is the same as the church has had through the centuries. We start with the printed Bibles we have today ... to show that they correspond with the printed Bible of the sixteenth century.... From these we can go back though the English and later versions to the fourth century. Then we can go back still farther and compare the use of Scripture in the writings of the [church] Fathers of the third century ... to the second century when versions in several languages are found. From this it is but a short step to the time of the apostles and the actual composition of the New Testament writings." (W. H. Griffith Thomas, *How We Got Our Bible*)

Literal Translation

KJV: "Cry and howl, son of man: for it shall be upon my people, it shall be upon all the princes of Israel: terrors by reason of the sword shall be upon my people: smite therefore upon thy thigh."

NASB: "Cry out and wail, son of man; for it is against My people, it is against all the officials of Israel. They are delivered over to the sword with My people, therefore strike [your] thigh."

Dynamic Equivalent (or thought-for-thought)

NIV: "Cry out and wail, son of man, for it is against my people; it is against all the princes of Israel. They are thrown to the sword along with my people. Therefore beat your breast."

NLT: "Son of man, cry out and wail; pound your thighs in anguish, for that sword will swallow my people and their leaders—everyone will die!"

Paraphrase

TLB: "Son of dust, with sobbing, beat upon your thigh, for that sword shall slay my people and all their leaders. All alike shall die."

Observations:

Now, go back to the beginning and review the translations of John 1:18, identifying paraphrases, literal and dynamic equivalents.

Gaining a Foothold

Translation work is laborious and must be done carefully. Wycliffe is a ministry that for decades has been translating the Scriptures into languages and dialects around the world. With each language group and culture, these workers labor to accurately translate the timeless truth of the gospel in words that each culture understands. In some cases they must help produce a written language, beginning with an alphabet, for a tribe or group that has only a verbal language. It takes many years to do this, in some cases twenty to thirty years to get the entire Bible into the language of a people who have no books.

Take a moment to pray for these people. We have over 400 English versions and kinds of Bibles. (A new study Bible is published every month!) Some people have no copy of the Word of God. Ask God to show you how you might help in this work.

Trailmarkers

✓ Look at Psalm 119:105 and memorize it together. Discuss how the Word lights up your path. What must we do to make sure that the lamp of the Word stays lit?

Teamwork

The purpose of this information is to grow your confidence, not to confuse you. Yes, there are many versions of the Bible, but the truth of the Word, and the power of the Holy Spirit acting through it, is what ultimately changes lives.

In light of the information in this session, take a few minutes to share Bible versions with others in the group. Then briefly work through the following as a guide to choosing a Bible.

1. What version reads best and would help you understand the Word in a clear way, particularly for devotional reading and meditation?

2. What version would you like to use for serious study?

3. Would you rather have a Bible with cross-references in the margin or none at all?

4. Would a study Bible with notes and explanations at the bottom of each page serve you best?

5. How about size?

6. Would you prefer a version with Jesus' words printed in red ink?

We have so many choices in our culture. Probably two versions should suffice, one for study (perhaps with notes), and one that is smaller and easy to use for daily devotional reading and travel. Chances are many of you already have a few versions. The important thing is to use them!

Reaching the Summit

As a result of this session, you should have an increased confidence in the accuracy and quality of the Bible you hold in your hands, while also understanding the range of translations available for your use and study. Ask any final questions you might have about this session.

Next Session

It's one thing to know where the Bible came from. But how do we know we can trust what it says? How do we know it is reliable? How do we know that anything we read is reliable?

In preparation for next session, bring in a copy of a newspaper or magazine article, or a short advertisement from the paper. You will decide as a group whether you can trust what it says.

Close in Prayer

Focus on praying for people you know who do not believe or understand the Bible, asking God to provide opportunities to speak with them after you have increased your confidence in the Word through this study.

Session 3

Reliability & Truth
Why We Can Trust Our Bible

The basis for trusting in the accuracy of Scripture.

Establishing Base Camp

Before I attended seminary, I worked for a Philadelphia bank, making the 45-minute commute each day on the train. One day I ran into an old football buddy from high school, John. He was reading a new book that described God's role in the universe. His father-in-law was a top leader in the Mormon church and had given him the book. Well, I was a fairly new Christian but had taken a Bible class or two in night school, so I began to ask him questions about what he was reading.

The discussions soon turned into friendly debates. John told me that the book was a fundamental leadership book for his belief system and was based on the teachings of Mormonism and the *Book of Mormon*. I asked him why he considered the *Book of Mormon* an accurate and reliable document. "Joseph Smith wrote it, based on a revelation from God," he said.

"How do you know?" I asked.

"First," he remarked, "we have Joseph Smith's testimony of what he saw and heard. Second, he was a trustworthy man. And, after all, everything in it is supported in the Bible!"

I decided to put my friend's logic and beliefs to the test, so I made a deal with him. "Do you believe the Bible is the Word of God?" I asked.

"Yes," he answered.

"Okay, we'll discuss your book," I said, "but we will compare what it says to the *Book of Mormon* and to Scripture. If your book or the *Book of Mormon* teaches something contrary to the Bible, and we both acknowledge that the Bible is from God, then that would mean the Mormon teaching is contradictory to the Bible, correct? And that Mormon teaching would be false. Reasonable to assume?" He agreed.

It did not take long to show John that the Bible teaches Jesus is the Son of God and possesses full humanity and full deity (see, for example, John 1:1-18; Philippians 2:6-11; Revelation 1:17). Mormonism teaches that Jesus was a human who worked his way up to "god status" and that we can do the same. Over the next several weeks our conversations went something like this.

"John, are you familiar with the Mormon material entitled *Doctrines and Covenants*?"

"Yes! It is great teaching!"

"It teaches that the Father has a body of flesh and bones. Right?" I asked.

"It does," he replied.

"Let's look at the Scripture. Could you read John 4:24 for me?" I handed him a Bible.

"God is Spirit and his worshipers must worship in spirit and truth" he read.

"Seems like we have a contradiction. Mormons teach God has a fleshly body and the Bible teaches he is Spirit," I remarked.

John was silent, then shuffled in his seat and smiled. "I suppose it depends on how you interpret it," he said.

His response was the same each time this happened. "That's your interpretation; I guess we just see it differently." I haven't seen him in fifteen years, but hope I raised enough doubts to cause him to look at Scripture. In any case, the Holy Spirit is going to have to break through some walls before he begins to see the truth plainly.

✓ If you brought an article or ad with you, take it out now. How do we determine the accuracy of something we read, a story we are told or something on TV? As a group, come up with a "reliability test" that you could apply to any statement of truth or any writing.

Mapping the Trail

✓ There are some incredible miracles and some seemingly strange occurrences in the Bible. Have you ever doubted the reliability of something you read in the Bible? If so, what was it?

You might be encouraged to know that there are some basic guidelines for determining the truth of any statement or document. Legal and criminal investigators use rigorous methods for determining truth and evaluating evidence. And we, as believers and students of the eternal and living Word of God, must be equally convinced that we have an accurate record of the works and words of the Creator. We will look at these in a few minutes.

✓ But first, consider: What standards or criteria would you use to determine the accuracy of the Bible? List them.

1.

2.

3.

4.

 ### Beginning the Ascent

Some years ago an atheist group published an advertisement for some of their literature. One book they were promoting, *The Bible Handbook*, was designed to supposedly refute the claims of Scripture. The ad stated: "Never again will you be unable to refute Christians. Everything is here: absurdities, indecencies, contradictions, unfulfilled prophecies, broken promises of god, . . . impossibilities, bad history . . ." (from *The American*

Atheist). I found it amusing, until I realized that there are people who will believe what they read in this book and never put the claims of the Bible to the test.

Let's look at what makes the Bible reliable and truthful. Ironically, there has been much less debate about the reliability of the Old Testament because of the meticulous nature with which the scribes copied manuscripts over the years. Though people debate the content and teachings, they do not debate the reliability of the documents. Most of the debate is focused on the New Testament because of the claims Jesus made to be God.

(*Note:* We have limited time in this small group setting and cannot provide an exhaustive treatment of this subject. For a more detailed treatment, see *The Case for Christ* by Lee Strobel. It addresses many of these issues in detail and has a wealth of other sources listed for your investigation.)

Tests of Reliability

Here are some ways to test the reliability of information in any ancient source, applied to the Bible.

1. The Character Test. What is the integrity and record of truthfulness of the individual providing the information? The Bible contains the testimony of eyewitnesses to events. But we must ultimately look to the credibility of the authors. Their stories contain accounts of their own lives (many not very flattering) and the events they witnessed. Their character is impeccable and attested to by others who knew them.

2. The Corroboration Test. Does the information given by eyewitnesses match up with other information reported on the same events? The disciples and writers of the New Testament speak and write with great conviction and clarity about Jesus. Historians of Jesus' time (the Jewish historian Josephus, who wrote in the late first century A.D., for example) mention the events of his life and ministry. Though they traveled and lived in different places, the accounts of what happened never contradict. The Bible is remarkably accurate and unified.

3. The Conviction Test. How strongly does the writer believe what he is writing? Is he or she willing to go "on trial" for the facts? We know that these writers and followers of Christ, whose lives we know from biblical

and nonbiblical history, went to their deaths proclaiming Christ and what he had done. Either they had
strong convictions based on what they had seen, or
they were part of a great hoax for which they were
willing to be tortured and killed.

    4. The Consistency Test. Does one section of litera-
ture compare favorably with another section on the
same content? Are there contradictions? Do the various
teachings by different authors support each other or do
they disagree? I think you will find that you can look at
sin, faith, love, justice, mercy, salvation, miracles and
God and find that each of these topics is discussed consistently throughout Scripture. This despite the fact that
it was written over 1,400 years by over forty authors
from different ethnic backgrounds living on three conti-
nents and from every walk of life! Fishermen and kings,
religious zealots and tax collectors, soldiers and shep-
herds, preachers and poets, Jews and Gentiles (even a
physician named Luke) contributed to the Bible. And
they present a clear and unified body of teaching.

    No one test alone is strong enough. For example,
anyone can have convictions and be sincerely wrong
or misinformed. And people with good character make mistakes. But
when you combine strong personal character, unwavering conviction,
corroborated evidence by multiple eyewitnesses (followers of Christ and
nonfollowers alike) and consistent treatment of subject matter, you have
a strong case for the reliability of the documents of the Old and New
Testaments.

    ✔ Why is it more important that the Bible be accurate than the
newspaper or some other literature? Why must we be so sure of
what it says? What is at stake?

Sanskrit professor Montiero-Williams, who studied Eastern books for over forty-two years, compares the Bible to the Eastern writings he has studied: "Pile them, if you will on the left side of your study table: but place your own Holy Bible on the right side—all by itself, all alone—and with a wide gap between them. For there is a great gulf between it and the so-called sacred books of the East which severs the one from the other utterly, hopelessly, and forever ... a veritable gulf which cannot be bridged over by any science of religious thought" (from Sidney Collett, *All About the Bible*).

Gaining a Foothold

The accuracy of the Bible is of utmost importance, especially the claims of Christ and the resurrection, as shown by 1 Corinthians 15:13-19:

> If there is no resurrection of the dead, then not even Christ has been raised. And if Christ has not been raised, our preaching is useless and so is your faith. More than that, we are then found to be false witnesses about God, for we have testified about God that he has raised Christ from the dead. But he did not raise him if in fact the dead are not raised. For if the dead are not raised, then Christ has not been raised either. And if Christ has not been raised, your faith is futile; you are still in your sins. Then those also who have fallen asleep in Christ are lost. If only for this life we have hope in Christ, we are to be pitied more than all men.

Trailmarkers

Read Luke 1:1-4. These verses are understood by scholars to be an introduction to both of his works—the Luke-Acts history of Christ and the church (see "Luke" in the *New Bible Dictionary* and the *New Bible Commentary*). He wrote more than one-third of the New Testament. Even though it's only two books, they are two of the largest by sheer volume.

✓ What is so significant about this statement by Luke?

Teamwork

This study and discussion can increase your confidence in the Word of God as you speak with others and obey it yourself. In smaller groups, try the following exercise.

A friend you know has been investigating Christianity and asks: "How you can you believe something as old as the Bible? Hasn't it changed so much over the years since it has been written? After all, there were no videos, TVs or printing presses. How can you be sure that what it says is true?" You have three options of how to respond.

1. Say, "Of all the questions I have ever heard, that sure is one of them!"

2. Ask, "What do you mean no TV? Haven't you ever watched *The Ten Commandments?*"

3. Provide a loving but clear response giving some information to help your friend understand how reliable the Bible actually is.

If you chose number three, pair off and take about ten minutes to create a response. Remember, you are not trying to "argue" but are rather trying to provide a confident answer.

When you come together, take five minutes and choose one of the subgroups to present their answer. Others should evaluate the response. Was it accurate? Was it tactful? How was the information from the study incorporated?

Reaching the Summit

Review the tests of reliability and how they build trust in the Bible. Identify any points for further growth or study.

Next Session

Who do you look to as an authority in the following areas? In preparation for the next session complete the following list:

1. Basketball_____
2. Computer technology_____
3. The Internet_____
4. Automobiles_____
5. Fashion_____
6. Current events_____
7. Education_____
8. Parenting_____
9. Music_____
10. Cooking_____

Be prepared to discuss what makes them an authority the next time.

Close in Prayer

Thank God for his Word and the confidence we can have in it. Ask the Holy Spirit to help you provide solid answers to those who have questions about the Bible.

Session 4

Authority
Why We Obey the Bible

Understanding the place of the Bible in our lives.

 ### Establishing Base Camp

I remember like it was yesterday. I can see the dusty field, smell the sweat, experience the exhaustion. Our high school football team had been humiliated the week before by a rival. We had performed poorly and were out of shape. After a two-hour practice, coach made us run forty-yard sprints. Usually we did ten to twelve. But this day we ran twenty-eight. It was grueling. I look back and think, *Why did we do this? Why didn't we all just go home after twelve?* Because we had submitted to the authority of a coach. When you are on the team, you do what the coach says. Even twenty-eight wind sprints.

Authority was paramount in Jesus' day. One day a Roman centurion asked Jesus to heal his sick and dying servant. He sent some Jewish leaders to ask Jesus to heal the man. While Jesus was on the way to the centurion's home, the soldier sent friends to intercept him. Picking up the story in Luke 7:6-10, the friends meet Jesus on the road and speak the words of the centurion to him:

> "Lord, don't trouble yourself, for I do not deserve to have you come under my roof. That is why I do not even consider myself worthy to come to you. But say the word and my servant will be healed. For I myself am a man under authority, with soldiers under me. I tell this one, 'Go,' and he goes; and that one, 'Come,' and he comes. I say to my servant, 'Do this,' and he does it."
>
> When Jesus heard this, he was amazed at him, and turning to the crowd following him, he said, "I tell you, I have not found such great faith even in Israel." Then the men who had been sent returned and found the servant well.

Reliability and authority are directly related. If information is unreliable, it can make no claim to authority. Last session we looked at the reliability of the Bible, the accuracy and authenticity of Scripture. This session we focus on authority. Many writings and teachings are reliable and accurate, but that does not mean we have to obey them, believe their claims or reorient our lives around them.

The Scriptures on the other hand call us to account for our values, decisions and beliefs. God has revealed himself in the Bible, and the thread of his authority is woven throughout the entire text. Jesus, who came to reveal God to us (John 1:18), claimed to be the Son of God and pegged each person's eternal destiny to faith in him (John 3:16-21; 11:25.)

Despite his claims, Jesus did not have to run around yelling, "I have authority! Listen to me!" His works and his words of truth were recognized as carrying authority. He spent much of his time preaching and teaching throughout Judea and Galilee. After he spoke, people said, "What is this teaching? With authority and power he gives orders to evil spirits and they come out!" (Luke 4:36).

✓ Did you fill in any names on the list at the end of last session? If so, choose one and describe why you think that person is recognized as an authority in their field. If not, look quickly now at the list and see who comes to mind.

Mapping the Trail

✓ If you have authority over someone (at work, school, in the military or with children) what do you expect from them?

✓ What might it take for you to become like the centurion, a "just say the word" Christ follower?

Beginning the Ascent

Read the following principles regarding the authority of Jesus and the Bible, and discuss the question after each one.

1. The Scripture speaks with authority. The Word of God calls people to obedience, thus claiming authority over our lives. Joshua said: "Do not let this Book of the Law depart from your mouth; meditate on it day and night, so that you may be careful to do everything written in it. Then you will be prosperous and successful" (Joshua 1:8). Jesus said, "Blessed are they who hear the Word of God and obey it!" (Luke 11:28). (For further study see also Exodus 20; Deuteronomy 30:16; Jeremiah 11:3-5; Psalm 119; Hebrews 4:12-13; 2 Peter 1:16-21.) In light of the authority of the Bible, what does this say about how we are to use it and treat it in our daily living?

2. Jesus speaks with authority. Jesus, the central focus of the Bible, commands obedience. He said, "Whoever has my commands and keeps them, he is the one who loves me. He who loves me will be loved by my Father, and I too will love him and show myself to him" (John 14:21). Why is it not arrogant for Jesus to make obedience a condition of love? After all, he could have said, "No matter what you do, I know that you still love me."

3. Jesus acts with authority. Jesus demonstrated his authority through miracles, signs and wonders (John 21:24-25), lived a life without sin (Hebrews 4:15) or wrongdoing (Luke 23:4), and claimed to speak only the truth (John 18:19-23). He exercised authority over Satan (Matthew 4:1-11), demons (Mark 5:1-20), death (John 11), nature (Luke 8:22-25), illness (Luke 4:38-39) and disease (Mark 5:25-34). If evil spirits, disease and nature obey Jesus without questioning his authority, why is it so difficult for us to obey him?

4. Jesus' authority calls believers into action in his name. After the resurrection Jesus stated his authority: "All authority in heaven and on earth has been given to me. Therefore go and make disciples of all nations, baptizing them in the name of the Father, and of the Son, and of the Holy Spirit, and teaching them to obey everything I have commanded you. And surely I am with you to the close of the age" (Matthew 28:18-20). This passage is commonly called the "Great Commission." Often people quote only verses 19-20, but the entire commission is based on verse 18. What is the scope and source of Jesus' authority? How does this influence how we should respond to this Great Commission?

5. Jesus' authority was observed by his followers. It is clear from the testimony of his followers that Jesus had authority as the Son of God. He did indeed perform miracles and rise from the dead (2 Peter 1:16-18; 1 John 1:1-4); and he spoke truth (John 21:24). How does Jesus' claim to deity affect his claim to having authority?

"In my own experience of more than 28 years of sharing the good news of the Savior with the academic world, I personally have never heard of a single individual—who has honestly considered the evidence—deny that Jesus Christ is the Son of God and the Savior of men. The evidence concerning the deity of the Lord Jesus Christ is overwhelmingly conclusive to any honest, objective seeker after truth. However, not all—not even the majority—of those to whom I have spoken have accepted Him as their Savior and Lord. This is not because they were *unable* to believe—they were simply *unwilling* to believe!" (Bill Bright, president of Campus Crusade, in the foreword to *Evidence That Demands a Verdict* by Josh McDowell

Gaining a Foothold

The Bible's authority (particularly as displayed in and through Jesus Christ) is not dependent on our acceptance of it. So we must choose to obey and respond to the authority of the Word, placing ourselves in a position of humility and willingness to respond as God commands.

✓ What areas of life are difficult for you to bring under the authority of the Word of God? Where or when is it most difficult for you to obey the commands of Christ?

Trailmarkers

✓ Memorize John 14:23 together or in pairs. If you cannot complete this now, at least get a firm grip on the powerful truth of this passage. What is the relationship between love and obedience?

✓ How does love produce obedience and obedience affirm love?

Teamwork

Read Philippians 2:5-11, and complete the following exercise.

1. Break into two groups. Have group A write down everything they see in the passage about authority and power. Have group B write down everything they observe about humility and servanthood.

2. Come back together and share your findings with the entire group.

3. Discuss how Jesus has been both master and servant in your life. Which is he today?

Reaching the Summit

Unlike many earthly authorities, the authority of the Word of God has integrity and character. And Jesus always exercises his authority in honorable and life-giving ways. So it is a great privilege to submit our will to God, knowing the great plans he has for us and the incredible future laid out for us in eternity. Take a few moments to reflect on the benefits of being under the authority of God's Word.

Next Session

Did you ever wonder how the books of the Bible were chosen? Or whether there are still some "lost books" out there? We will cover that in the next session. To prepare, you might try memorizing the books of the Bible from Genesis to Revelation. This will help you find your way around the Bible as you look up references and follow the pastor's sermon or class.

Close in Prayer

Pray for each other to have a deeper conviction to obey the Word of God. Confess any rebellious attitudes toward authority and ask the Holy Spirit to work in your life to challenge you to greater obedience and trust.

Session 5

Canon
What Books Were Included & Why
Understanding the total written revelation of God to us.

 ### Establishing Base Camp

Years ago, when I was watching Billy Graham in an interview, he was asked how to defend the faith. The commentator asked Graham, "With so much false teaching present these days, how do you keep up with all the cults and sects? You certainly must study them carefully so you can refute them."

Graham responded, "Not really. I asked experts at the Department of Treasury a similar question when I toured the facility. 'How do you know a counterfeit bill when you see one?' They answered, 'We spent hundreds of hours studying the authentic bill. After that, it is easy to spot a fraud.' So that's how I can spot error in teachings about the Bible. Know the real thing and you can spot an error a mile away."

Let's apply Graham's teaching to the following: What if you were to open your Bible and read this story from Jesus' childhood years?

> Now Jesus made of that clay 12 sparrows: and it was the Sabbath day. And a child ran and told Joseph, saying, "Behold, your child plays about the brook, and has made sparrows of the clay, which is not lawful (on the Sabbath)." And he, when he heard it, went and said to the child, "Why have you done this and profaned the Sabbath?" But Jesus answered him not, but looked upon the sparrows and said, "Go, take your flight, and remember me in your life." And at the word they took flight and went up into the air. And when Joseph saw it he was astonished.

✓ **What strikes you as odd about this story? Does this story sound true? Why or why not?**

Mapping the Trail

"CNN NEWS FLASH! A group of archaeologists has just discovered what they believe to be a lost book of the Bible just outside Jerusalem. It looks like an old manuscript, feels like an old manuscript and is signed by someone called 'The Rock' at the bottom of the last page! It is believed to be a work by Peter!"

✓ If such an account were broadcast and you were asked to consider including this new book in the Bible, what would you do? What "tests" would you apply to it to determine if it belonged with the rest of Scripture?

"Acceptance of the Bible as the infallible written Word of God entails prior historical conclusions as to which books constitute Scripture. Some branches of the Christian church—e.g., Roman Catholic, Eastern Orthodox—include more than 66 books in the canon. Some modern sects—e.g., Mormonism, Christian Science—claim extrabiblical revelation. Muslims believe that God revealed the Koran to Muhammad from heaven, word for word. So the question of canonization (how we inherited the precise contents of our Bible) becomes a vital one for Christian faith and practice." (Milton Fischer, *Expositor's Bible Commentary*)

Beginning the Ascent

In this session we will focus on how and why the books of the Bible were recognized as Scripture. After all, there were other writers at the time who claimed to hear from God (like the people who wrote the *Gospel of Thomas,* which is excerpted above).

Definition of Canon

Transliterated from the Greek word *kanon,* which means "a builder's rule," a canon is a body of authoritative literature. The canon of Scripture is the sixty-six books recognized as the Word of God, the Bible (see the *New Bible Dictionary*). They were measured as accurate and from God, thus qualifying to be called *Scripture.*

We do not assign authority to the Bible or choose Scripture; we recognize inherent authority in the text itself and affirm that it is indeed Scripture.

Scripture was a special term in the days of the Christ. It referred to sacred writings, not simply any writings. In fact, it was used only in reference to the Old Testament writings (the only Bible in Jesus' time).

Why Bother with a Canon?

There are at least three reasons for having a system for acknowledging the writings of Scripture as authoritative and from God.

1. False teaching. Remember, there were no printing presses or computers. Everything was communicated by word of mouth or words on parchments (in books and scrolls). Anyone could claim to have a message from God. Though it was clear that the Scriptures were doctrinally sound, the early church had to defend itself against heresy in the form of false teachers and false writers.

As a group, look at 2 Peter 2:1-3; 1 John 4:1-3; Jude 3-4. Why do these writers have such a sense of urgency?

2. Use of the Scriptures in worship services. Early Christians needed to be certain that what they were using was actually from God and brought glory to his name.

3. Persecution. In the days of the early church, there existed intense and widespread persecution of believers. Often targeted were leaders (pastors, teachers) and the Scriptures. Ray Petry, in his *History of Christianity*, describes the horrible situation under Emperor Diocletian at around A.D. 300.

> New Testament scholar F. F. Bruce has said, "One thing must be emphatically stated. The New Testament books did not become authoritative for the Church because they were formally included in a canonical list; on the contrary, the Church included them in her canon because she already regarded them as divinely inspired, recognizing their innate worth and generally apostolic authority, direct or indirect. The first ecclesiastical (church) councils to classify the canonical books were both held in North Africa—at Hippo Regius in A.D. 393 and at Carthage in A.D. 397—but what these councils did was not to impose something new upon the Christian communities but to codify what was already the general practice of these communities." (*The New Testament Documents*)

This was the nineteenth year of the reign of Diocletian, in Dystrus (which the Romans call March), when the feast of the Saviour's passion was near a hand, and royal edicts were published everywhere, commanding that the churches should be razed to the ground, the Scriptures destroyed by fire, those who held positions of honor degraded, and the household servants, if they persisted in the Christian profession, be deprived of their liberty.

Then as the first decrees were followed by others commanding that those in prison should be set free, if they would offer sacrifice [to the Emperor], but those who refused should be tormented with countless tortures. (vol. 1, p. 54)

To be willing to endure imprisonment or torture, these believers wanted to be sure they had the authentic Word of God.

Tests of the Canon

Refer back to "Mapping the Trail" and compare the tests you discussed there with those that follow. There were three major tests used by the church to fend off heretical writings or other religious writings that simply did not measure up to the divine character of the Scriptures. Writings had to pass all three tests or they were not Scripture.

1. Apostolic origin. By the time of the New Testament, the Old Testament had been accepted by Jews as the authoritative Word of God. The events had been witnessed and the writers (like Moses, David and the prophets) were revered and had spoken from God. An Old Testament prophet who misrepresented God was to be stoned (Deuteronomy 18:20-22).

So in the New Testament an apostle or someone closely associated with an apostle had to be the source. The apostles, taught and commissioned by Christ, were considered the official mouthpieces of God. (See Matthew 28:18-20. Even Paul, who had met the resurrected Christ on the Damascus road in Acts 9, met these criteria.)

The only nonapostles to write in the New Testament were Luke (who traveled extensively with Paul and, in effect, recorded Paul's ministry), Mark (who accompanied Peter and recorded his preaching, 1 Peter 5:13) and Jude who was Jesus' half-brother and among the early followers of Christ.

2. Doctrinal soundness. Did the writing square up with the teachings of Christ, the teachings of other apostles and the teachings of the Old Testament Scriptures? If not, it was not considered Scripture.

3. Recognition by the church. Early church councils and leadership gatherings were sometimes devoted to doctrinal issues. It was clear to these leaders that the thirty-nine Old Testament books and twenty-seven New Testament books were the only writings that could be called Scripture.

✔ Go back and apply these tests to the quote from the *Gospel of Thomas.* Does it pass all of the tests?

✔ What standards or guidelines must be met in your work? Or what standard do you have for your kids? What role do standards play in our lives?

Gaining a Foothold

There were two categories of writing not included in the canon, but sometimes they appear in Bibles from other faiths or traditions. These are the Apocrypha (hidden writings) and the pseudepigrapha (false writings).

1. The Apocrypha includes the following:

1 Esdras	Letters of Jeremiah
2 Esdras	Prayer of Azariah and the Three Young Men
Tobit	Susanna
Judith	Bel and the Dragon
Additions to Esther	Prayer of Manasseh
Wisdom of Solomon	1 Macabees
Baruch	2 Macabees
Ecclesiasticus (Sirach)	

Though considered of some value because they provide some history and insights into the four hundred years between the Old and New Testaments, they do not meet the tests of the canon. They were written in the last two centuries before Christ, during an uprising of the Jews against a oppressive government led by Antiochus IV. The books contain stories and fanciful tales, and some inaccurate history.

2. Pseudepigrapha (or the apocryphal New Testament) include:

Apocalypse of Peter

Acts of Paul and Thecla

Acts of Pilate

Epistle to the Laodiceans

Gospel of the Hebrews

Gospel of Philip

Gospel of Thomas (quoted at the beginning of the session)

Again, these books were written late by suspect authors who claimed to have had contact with the disciples. These works and many others never met the tests. Most include stories and material devoid of spiritual worth, no eyewitnesses and in contradiction with the sixty-six books of Scripture. A "no-brainer" for the early church leaders.

Jerome, the historian who in A.D. 400 translated the Bible into Latin (called the *Vulgate*), stated his concern regarding including the Apocrypha along with the Hebrew Old Testament books. "Jerome insisted that it is only the Hebrew books which are canonical or scriptural.... He had grasped the important principle that the Old Testament Scriptures are entrusted to the Jews (Rom 3:2, 9:4) and that the Christian church has no right to add any books not recognized by them" (*Harper's Concise Book of Christian Faith*, p. 39).

Trailmarkers

Memorize 2 Timothy 3:16 and discuss the importance of this verse.

Teamwork

Look up these verses and see what insights you can gain about the Scripture and why the early church said that the authority of the books lies in the books themselves.

✓ 1 Timothy 5:18: By quoting Deuteronomy 25:4 and Luke 10:7, what is Paul saying about Luke's teaching?

✓ 1 Thessalonians 2:13: What is the "word of God" Paul is referring to?

✓ 2 Peter 3:15-16: How does Peter describe Paul's writings?

✓ Revelation 22:18-19: What does this say about the finality of the biblical record? Compare it with Jude 3-4.

Reaching the Summit

You have come a long way on a tough subject. The canon can sound like a boring subject until you realize it answers questions like "Who decided what goes in the Bible? Why does your Bible not have the Apocrypha? How do you know that some other books don't exist?" Discuss any final questions or express interests for further study.

Next Session

Come prepared to do an exciting, challenging team project.

Close in Prayer

Take a moment to thank God for his Word, and for those who suffered and worked to make sure it was protected, preserved and revered. Pray for each other and celebrate what you have learned.

Session 6

Putting It All Together

Establishing Base Camp

This session we want to draw on all that you have learned from sessions one through five. If you missed a session, it is fine because this is a group project and others can help you.

Are there any loose ends you want to tie together from previous sessions? If so, discuss those now. Feel free to review notes and material from the study guide.

Teamwork

Years ago when I was in Dallas training leaders in churches, my partner and I came across an opinion column written by a pastor (let's call him *Dave*) of a church in the city of Fort Worth. He was critical of the Bible, saying that it was a good moral storybook (like *Aesop's Fables*) but filled with errors and stories that no intelligent person could believe.

Here is Dave's basic reasoning. As I summarize what he wrote, I will write as if he is speaking.

> If you think the Bible is without errors and the stories are true, then you have to believe that God dictated it to the apostles and prophets and that they had no part in it. But if they did have a part (which, of course, they did), then it must be filled with human errors. There are three reasons why you can't believe that the Bible is totally true in all it teaches.
>
> 1. God is Spirit; he writes no words to us. We have assigned human characteristics to God, and therefore we believe he speaks in a way that we understand, like the English language. But God is always speaking to us in different and unique ways.
>
> 2. The writers of the book of Exodus believed that God sent plagues to kill Egyptians—even babies—simply because they were not God's chosen peo-

ple (as were the Jews). I find it hard to believe that God murders his little babies. The Jews simply thought of themselves as God's favorites, and everyone else was their enemy.

3. What do you make of the book of Jonah? You cannot possibly believe that Jonah was swallowed by a whale, escaped being chewed up, found oxygen for three days and then was disgorged on dry land in Nineveh. The book is a great story reminding us that a journey away from God is a rocky road, and you'd better turn around or you will be swallowed up in eternal darkness.

We do not have time to address all the issues raised here, because some involve interpretation methods, but we can address the issues that correspond to what we have been studying. (For more information see the Bible 101 guide *Interpretation.*) So, in thirty minutes, answer the questions below as you draft a response to Dave. Then come together for discussion. The goal is not to be able to simply prove Dave wrong and feel smug. Rather, we want to give a 1 Peter 3:15 response to critics and doubters of the faith, gaining confidence in what and whom we put our faith.

1. In the first paragraph Pastor Dave states that in order to believe the Bible is accurate you must believe that God "dictated" the words to people who acted like nonthinking robots as they wrote them down. Using what you studied about revelation and inspiration, how would you respond to that?

2. He states that God doesn't use words but that he still speaks to us constantly. Does this seem like a contradiction? If you were God and wanted to communicate to people who spoke and wrote in words, how would you communicate with them? How might Dave respond to the teaching we had about the reliability of the Bible?

3. Since Dave does not believe in the judgment of God and views God only as kind and gentle, he cannot accept the biblical stories that describe God's wrath. His wrath and hatred of sin are clearly taught in the Bible, as is his compassion (both evident in Exodus 34:6-7). If Dave lets his perception of God determine which parts of the Bible to believe, then what is his view of the authority of the Bible?

4. Finally, Dave challenges the Bible head-on. Given what he says about the book of Jonah, how might you respond? Use your study of the canon in your answer.

Reaching the Summit

You have discovered how the Word of God came to us. It is an amazing process, protected by God all these years so that each generation can have the eternal, powerful, truthful, authoritative, life-giving Scripture in hand. You probably have more questions along with your answers. A good Bible dictionary or encyclopedia can handle most of these.

Next Session

Discuss whether you want to continue with the Bible 101 series or begin some other study.

Close in Prayer

Spend some time in prayers of gratitude, but also leave plenty of time for other group needs.

Leader's Notes

Few ventures are more defining than leading a group that produces changed lives and sharper minds for the cause of Christ. At Willow Creek we have seen small groups transform our church, offer deeper levels of biblical community and provide an environment where truth can be understood and discussed with enthusiasm. So we have focused on a group-based study rather than a classroom-lecture format or individual study (though these studies can profitably be used in both settings with minor adaptations.)

Each method of learning has its strengths; each has its weaknesses. In personal study one can spend as little or as much time on an issue and can focus specifically on personal needs and goals. The downside: there is no accountability to others, no one to challenge thoughts or assumptions, no one to provide support when life comes tumbling down around you. The classroom is ideal for proclaiming truth to many at one time and for having questions answered by those with expertise or knowledge in a subject area. But the pace of the class depends largely on the teacher, and there is limited time to engage in the discussion of personal issues. The small group is optimal for life-on-life encouragement, prayer and challenge. And it provides a place where learning is enhanced through the disciplines of biblical community. But small groups are usually not taught by content experts and cannot focus solely on one person's needs.

Our hope is that you will be able to use this curriculum in a way that draws from the best of all three methods. Using the small group as a central gathering place, personal preparation and study will allow you to focus on your own learning and growth goals. The small group activity will provide you with an engaging environment for refining your understanding and gaining perspective into the lives and needs of others. And perhaps by inviting a knowledgeable outsider to the group (or a cluster of small groups at a Saturday seminar, for example) you could gain the benefits of solid teaching in a given subject area. In any case your devotion to Christ, your commitment to your local church and your obedience to the Word of God are of utmost importance to us. Our desire is to see you "grow in the grace and knowledge of the Lord Jesus Christ."

Leadership Tips

Here are some basic guidelines for leaders. For more extensive leadership support and training we recommend that you consult *The Willow Creek Guide to Leading Lifechanging Small Groups,* where you will find many suggestions for leading creative groups.

Using the leader's notes. The questions in the study will not be repeated in the leader's notes. Instead, we have provided comments, clarifications, additional information, leadership tips or group exercises. These will help you guide the discussion and keep the meeting on track.

Shared leadership. When leading a small group remember that your role is to guide the discussion and help draw people into the group process. Don't try to be the expert for everything. Seek to involve others in the leadership process and activities of group life (hosting meetings, leading prayer, serving one another, leading parts of the discussion and so forth).

Preparation. Your work between meetings will determine group effectiveness during meetings. Faithful preparation does not mean that you will control the meeting or that it will move exactly as you planned. Rather, it provides you with a guiding sense of the desired outcomes of the time together so that you can gauge the pace of the meeting and make adjustments along the way. Above all, make sure you are clear about the overall goal of the meeting. Then, even if you get appropriately sidetracked dealing with a personal concern or a discussion of related issues, you can graciously help the group refocus on the goal of the meeting. Also, preparation will allow you to observe how others are engaging with the material. *You should complete the study* before coming to the meeting. You can participate in the group activities at the meeting, but take time to become personally acquainted with the material in case you need to alter the schedule or amount of time on each section.

Purpose. The series is designed to help people understand the Word and be confident in their ability to read, study and live its life-changing truths. Bible 101 is not designed for a group whose primary goal is caregiving or support. That does not mean you will avoid caring for each other, praying for needs or supporting one another through personal crises. It simply means that the *entire* focus of the group is not for these purposes. At the same time, the content should never take precedence over the process of transformation. There will be appropriate times to set the curriculum aside and pray. Or you may want to spend an evening having fun together. Remember, Jesus did not say, "Go therefore into all the world and complete the curriculum." Our focus is to make disciples. The curriculum is a tool, not a master. Use it consistently and with discernment, and your group will be well-served. But be clear about the primary focus of the group as you gather, and remind people every few weeks about the core purpose so that the group does not drift. So even though this is designed for six meetings per study guide, you might take longer if you have a meeting that focuses entirely on prayer or service.

Length of Meeting. We assume that you have about seventy to ninety minutes for this meeting, including prayer and some social time. If you have more or less time, adjust accordingly, especially if you have a task-based group. In that case, since you must complete the task (working on a ministry team or serving your church in some way), you will have to be selective in what you cover unless you can devote at least one hour to the meeting. In the format described below, feel free to play with the time allowed for "Beginning the Ascent," "Trailmarkers" and "Teamwork." We have given general guidelines for time to spend on each section. But depending on the size of group (we recommend about eight members), familiarity with the Bible and other group dynamics, you will have to make adjustments. After a few meetings you should have a good idea of what it will take to accomplish your goals.

Format. We have provided you with a general format. But feel free to provide some creativity or a fresh approach. You can begin with prayer, for example, or skip the "Establishing Base Camp" group opener and dive right into the study. We recommend that you follow the format closely early in the group process. As your group and your leadership skills mature and progress, you should feel increasing freedom to bring your creativity and experience to the meeting format. Here is the framework for the format in each of the guides in this series.

 Establishing Base Camp

This orients people to the theme of the meeting and usually involves a group opener or icebreaker. Though not always directly related to the content, it will move people toward the direction for the session. A base camp is the starting point for any mountain journey.

 Mapping the Trail

In this component we get clear about where we will go during the meeting. It provides an overview without giving away too much and removing curiosity.

 Beginning the Ascent

This is the main portion of the meeting: the climb toward the goal. It is the teaching and discussion portion of the meeting. Here you will find questions and explanatory notes. You will usually find the following two components included.

Pullouts. These provide additional detail, clarification or insight into content or questions that may arise in the participants' minds during the session.

Charts/Maps. Visual learners need more than words on a page. Charts, maps and other visuals combined with the content provide a brief, concise summary of the information and how it relates.

Gaining a Foothold

Along the trail people can drift off course or slip up in their understanding. These footholds are provided for bringing them into focus on core issues and content.

 Trailmarkers

These are key biblical passages or concepts that guide our journey. Participants will be encouraged to memorize or reflect on them for personal growth and for the central biblical basis behind the teaching.

 Teamwork

This is a group project, task or activity that builds a sense of community and shared understanding. It will be different for each study guide and for each lesson, depending on the author's design and the purpose of the content covered.

 Reaching the Summit

This is the end of the content discussion, allowing members to look back on what they have learned and capture it in a brief statement or idea. This "view from the top" will help them once again focus on the big picture after spending some time on the details.

Balancing caregiving and study/discussion. One of the most difficult things to do in a group, as I alluded to above, is balancing the tension between providing pastoral and mutual care to members and getting through the material. I have been in small groups where needs were ignored to get the work done, and I have been in groups where personal needs were the driving force of the group to the degree that the truth of the Word was rarely discussed. These guides are unique because they are designed to train and teach processes that must take place in order to achieve its purpose. But the group would fail miserably if someone came to a meeting and said, "I was laid off today from my job," and the group said a two-minute prayer and then opened their curriculum. So what do you do? Here are some guidelines.

1. People are the most important component of the group. They have real needs. Communicate your love and concern for people, even if they don't always get all the work done or get sidetracked.

2. When people disclose hurts or problems, address each disclosure with empathy and prayer. If you think more time should devoted to someone, set aside time at the end of the meeting, inviting members to stay for additional prayer or to console the person. Cut the meeting short by ten minutes to accomplish this. Or deal with it right away for ten to fifteen minutes, take a short break, then head into the study.

3. Follow up with people. Even if you can't devote large portions of the meeting time to caregiving, you and others from the group can provide this between meetings over the phone or in other settings. Also learn to leverage your time. For example, if your meeting begins at 7:00 p.m., ask the member in need and perhaps one or two others from the group to come at 6:30 p.m. for sharing and prayer. A person will feel loved, your group will share in the caregiving, and it is not another evening out for people.

4. Assign prayer partners or groups of three to be little communities within the group. Over the phone or on occasional meetings outside the group (before church and so on) they could connect and check in on how life is going.

5. For serious situations solicit help from others, including pastors or other staff at church. Do not go it alone. Set boundaries for people with serious care needs, letting them know that the group can devote some but not substantial meeting time to support them. "We all know that Dave is burdened by his son's recent illness, so I'd like to spend the first ten minutes tonight to lift him up in prayer and commit to support Dave through this season. Then, after our meeting I'd like us to discuss any specific needs you (Dave) might have over the next two to three weeks (such as meals, help with house chores, etc.) and do what we can to help you meet those needs." Something to that effect can keep the group on track but still provide a place to express compassion.

Take time to look at the entire series if you have chosen only one of the guides. Though each can be used as a stand-alone study, there is much to benefit from in the other guides because each covers material essential for a complete overview of how to study and understand the Bible. We designed the guides in series form so that you can complete them in about a year if you meet weekly, even if you take a week off after finishing each guide.

A Word About Leadership

One of your key functions as a small group leader is to be a cheerleader—someone who seeks out signs of spiritual progress in others and makes some noise about it. What have you seen God doing in your group members' lives as a result of this study? Don't assume they've seen that progress—and definitely don't assume they are beyond needing simple words of encouragement. Find ways to point out to people the growth you've seen. Let them know it's happening, and that it's noticeable to you and others.

There aren't a whole lot of places in this world people's where spiritual progress is going to be recognized and celebrated. After all, wouldn't you like to hear someone say somthing like that to you? Your group members feel the same way. You have the power to make a profound impact through a sincere, insightful remark.

Be aware also that some groups get sidetracked by a difficult member or situation that hasn't been confronted. And some individuals could be making significant progress, but they just need a nudge. "Encouragement" is not about just saying "nice" things; it's about offering *words that urge*. It's about giving courage (en-*courage*-ment) to those who lack it.

So leaders, take a risk. Say what needs to be said to encourage your members as they grow in their knowledge of the Bible. Help them not just amass more information, but move toward the goal of becoming fully devoted followers of Jesus Christ. Go ahead; make their day!

Session 1. How We Got Our Bible: Revelation & Inspiration.

Overview the Guide (1 min.) These six sessions will give you a firm grasp on the process and significance of how God's Word came to the printed pages of the Bible. You will learn how God speaks, how the original writings of Scripture came into being, why we have the books we have and why the Bible is reliable and authoritative for our lives. Your confidence in the Word of God will grow and your passion for studying it will come to life.

Introduce the Session (1 min.) Introduce the purpose and goal.

Purpose: This session is designed to explain the process of how the Bible we hold in our hands came into existence. This will increase our confidence in the

Word of God and help us describe to seeking friends or challenging foes that the Scriptures are indeed the Word of God.

Goal: To be able to explain the process of how we got our present Bible, particularly the role of *revelation* (how God reveals himself to us) and *inspiration* (the process by which God communicated to the writers of Scripture. We want to foster confidence in the Word through familiarity with how we were given the Scriptures.

Establishing Base Camp (10 min.) The Holy Spirit guided the process and content of writing the Scripture, ensuring that there was no error but allowing the writers to use their own writing styles and personalities. These questions are designed to give people real-life examples of how a guide leads, directs and protects without treating people like robots. You will soon see that the Holy Spirit functioned in much the same way in the process of bringing Scripture to us.

Mapping the Trail (10 min.) Help members see that few people really understand how the Bible came into being. This will give us greater confidence as we read the Bible and as we point others to its truths.

Beginning the Ascent (30 min.) Walk your group through the definitions and the chart "How We Got Our Bible." Look up the verses listed in the definitions. Ask members to each look up a couple of the verses.

General Revelation: Because these passages are longer, you might break your small group up into subgroups, one for each passage. Take just a few minutes to read each passage and debrief the key truth the group has discovered.

Special Revelation: Help the group distinguish between specific and general revelation. Give the group a test to see if they understand the difference: Which of the following is specific revelation and which is general revelation?

☐ Saul of Tarsus is blinded by light in Acts 9, and Jesus speaks to him.

☐ A beautiful sunset on the beach.

The first is specific, the second is general and available to everyone to see or experience.

Inspiration: These are God's words spoken trhough people and protected by the Spirit. By contrast, an author who is "inspired" to write a poem is emotionally motivated, and inspiration comes from within. The words are the author's, not God's.

Manuscript: Important here is the fact that the words God wanted written were painstakingly written and copied in such a way as to maintain absolute accuracy of the text. We will cover this process next session, so delay any questions that arise here.

Translation: There are currently over four hundred versions of the English Bible translation, plus translations into other languages around the world.

Walk your group through the overview chart again. The goal is ultimately to have each member of the group be able to look at the chart and, in his or her own words, walk someone through the process of how the Bible came to us, including some supporting Scriptures.

Gaining a Foothold (5 min.) Read this to your group.

Trailmarkers (10 min.) This can be done as a group or in smaller groups for more participation. But here are a few comments about these verses.

2 Timothy 3:16-17: When Paul used the word *Scripture* he was referring to the Old Testament and probably his own writings. For instance, Peter calls Paul's writing Scripture in 2 Peter 3:15-16.

2 Peter 1:20-21: Peter claims that he was an eyewitness of Jesus' life and ministry. He is validating the claims of his apostolic preaching and refers to the fact that no prophecy of Scripture was the result of humanity alone, but rather a process guided by the Holy Spirit. So in effect he says, "My prophetic teaching is not from me alone; God's Spirit is guiding me." Mark recorded the preaching and teaching of Peter in the gospel of Mark, thus implying that it too is Scripture.

Scripture was a sacred term, only used by people when referring to the writings of the Word of God.

Teamwork (15 min.) You might use role-play with this exercise with one or two people after you have had time to put some thoughts together. Let someone take the role of the woman on the plane. The other person should take three to four minutes to present an answer to her. Then have the group provide feedback.

Reaching the Summit (5 min.) Try giving one definition to each group member, asking them to state the definition in their own words. Ask one other person to give feedback. Again the point here is to encourage each other and not pick apart everyone's definition. Let them know "we're all in this together," trying to help each other be clear and confident about the truth of the Word of God.

Next Session (3 min.) Encourage members to look at different Bible versions that we have listed. There can be a lot of confusion as to why there are so many available, and we want to help people become confident with the range of versions. Ask who has different versions, and see if they can bring them next meeting.

Close in Prayer (10 min.) Thank God for the clarity of his Word and for speaking to his people in ways that we can understand his love for us. You might pair up for prayer this session so people can begin to get to know someone a little better. You can close the meeting with a brief prayer of blessing for the group.

Session 2. How We Got Our Bible: Manuscripts & Translations.

Introduce the Session (1 min.) Go over the purpose and goal with the group.

Purpose: To understand how we got our Bible, continuing from last session, with particular emphasis on the development of the manuscripts and the translations.

Goal: To be able to describe the process of how the Word came into print and to be able to discern the differences between various Bible translations and versions.

Establishing Base Camp (10 min.) Read the illustration together and help people get a sense of the need for an accurate translation, but also for some of the issues involved. Ultimately translation into English affects the kinds of Bible versions we have, a few of which are probably represented in your group.

Discuss the questions listed and focus on the need for accuracy. Can we be certain our Bible is accurate?

Mapping the Trail (10 min.) Make observations about the different versions. Later in the session we will talk about how these translations are different and why. For now, see what observations the group can make. Notice especially:

KJV: King James English sounds to some people more reverent and to others just old-fashioned or formal.

NRSV: This version ensures gender-neutral language when that is assumed. Here "no man" is rendered "no one" because this is true of all people, not just men. The NRSV does this throughout their translation.

NASB: Italicized words in the NASB mean that this word was not in the original Greek, but the grammar implies a word and the English requires one. From the context the obvious word is *him*.

NLT: Notice how the NLT has included "Son" and "who is himself God" so that the reader is clear that the Son is also deity. Rather than choose one reading (like NIV or NASB) both are included.

NIV: Note that *bosom* is rendered *side* in this version. We rarely say bosom today, but the NASB and KJV are trying to remain true to the actual wording. However, the meaning is lost a little. The use of *God* instead of *Son* is a decision based on manuscripts we have in our possession that the KJV translators did not have when they wrote.

Note: Some Christians believe there is a "KJV-only" Bible translation. All other modern translations are suspect to them. Only the KJV is the real Bible. This is not the time to discuss this issue, except to acknowledge that the KJV is based on manuscripts available at the time it was translated. Hundreds of years of archaeological work has yielded manuscripts from earlier in history. When translators have many copies of a biblical text at their disposal, they usually use the earliest manuscripts, those closest in time to the events that took place. A copy from A.D. 300 would take precedence over a copy from A.D. 900 of the same text. So, if there is a word or letter that is different between two manuscripts, the translators would assume the earlier version was more accurate.

The logic behind this states that later manuscripts have more chances for errors or changes as scribes, in some cases, varied a word that they thought had been mistranslated in an earlier copy.

TLB and AMP: These are more free in their choice of words. The Message and TLB are paraphrases. The AMP is a unique version, adding explanations and alternate translation options right in the text, sometimes in brackets or parentheses. The developers of this version knew that words have a range of meanings, and translators must sometimes choose one word from perhaps three or four, any of which would be an accurate translation. So they include several of the options or an explanation of a word right in the text.

Beginning the Ascent (30 min.) Ask a couple members to walk your group through the chart, providing some explanations along the way. Tell them they can call on anyone in the group to help if they get stuck, and they can ask anyone in the group to provide a definition of any term on the chart. This makes for some fun and helpful review.

Manuscript: When discussing this, it is important to emphasize that the words God wanted written were painstakingly transcribed and copied in such a way as to maintain absolute accuracy of the text. The scribes who copied the original texts were trained to destroy manuscripts if, while proofing the copy, even a single error was discovered. In addition, we have over 5,000 copies of manuscripts of the New Testament alone, and thousands more of the Old Testament (thousands more than we have of any other ancient literature).

So if critics want to challenge the historical accuracy of the text, they must likewise debate the reliability of every other historical matter recorded in this way (writings from Rome, Egypt, Babylon, China and so forth). There is more evidence for the Bible's accuracy in transmission than there is for any other ancient literature. If members want to explore this more fully, they can consult *The Case for Christ* by Lee Strobel or *The Books and the Parchments* by F. F. Bruce.

Here is some information designed to give you confidence in discussing the reliability of the biblical documents compared to the existing works we have by other ancient writers.

Author	Work	Date Written	Earliest Copy We Possess	# Copies
Homer	Iliad	no date	no date	643
Herodutus	History	400 B.C.	A.D. 900	8
Plato	Various	400 B.C.	A.D. 900	7
Aristotle	Various	300 B.C.	A.D. 300	5
Livy	Roman History	A.D. 30	A.D. 900	20
	New Testament	A.D. 100	A.D. 200	5,400

If scholars consider Homer's *Iliad* so accurate, and it is written 800 B.C., why not the New Testament? And if we rely on only twenty copies of Livy's *Roman History* when the earliest copy we have is 900 years after the events took place, and we have only twenty copies, then we must see the New Testament as even more reliable.

You may want to read the following to the group: Scholar F. F. Bruce, writing in *The New Testament Documents: Are They Reliable?* says, "There is no body of ancient literature in the world which enjoys such a wealth of textual attestation as the New Testament." In plain English, "No document in history has as many accurate manuscripts as the New Testament!"

Translation: When reading the various translations of Ezekiel 21:12, notice how the literal translations keep the original Hebrew idiom "strike the thigh" or "smite the thigh" which in Hebrew times meant to bring shame or anguish (see *thigh* in the *New Bible Dictionary*). The NIV, translating based on dynamic equivalent, renders it "beat your breast," a more English-friendly expression of the idiom, but still translating original words in the rest of the verse. And notice how the TLB paraphrase leaves out much of the original wording and conveys the sense of what is happening. After reviewing Ezekiel 21:12 with everyone and comparing translations, return to "Mapping the Trail" and show people how John 1:18 is translated in each version.

Take time to discuss any questions people might have about manuscripts or translations. It can be rather technical material, at least on the surface. But the result of studying should be a confidence in the Bible and an ability to handle basic questions people might have about it. After all, in many places, we are known as "people of the book," and it is important to know why the Bible is so unique.

Gaining a Foothold (10 min.) Read this to your group and spend a few moments praying. It is easy for prosperous Westerners to treat translation of the Bible as a relatively mundane issue, but for many cultures, having one copy of the Bible (or even the New Testament) would mean everything!

 Trailmarkers (10 min.) You might want to read a few other verses in the Psalm, for example, 119:65-72. There are so many great verses about God's Word! I have chosen a popular verse for memorization, but for those who have already memorized it, try 119:9 and 11.

After some memory work, which can be done with partners, discuss what it means that the Word lights our path. How should we treat this Word of God if it is the light of our path? What does this mean for everyday living?

If anyone asks, Psalm 119 is divided into 22 sections, each named after a letter in the Hebrew alphabet. The first letter of each line in a section begins with the same letter of the alphabet. For example, if we did this in English, the first word in every line of section one would begin with A, each line in section two would begin with B and so on. It was easier to memorize this way.

Teamwork (15 min.) This exercise can be organized in various ways, but is probably done best in groups of three or four. Let people give opinions and help each other make some choices. You might have some samples with you (like a *The NIV Study Bible,* a Bible without red letter or references, a New Testament and so on). Or you could ask members ahead of time to bring such items for you. Allow people to complete the process, then come together and share the results.

Reaching the Summit (5 min.) Review basic definitions and concepts from this session. Encourage members to ask others they know questions like "What is your impression of the Bible? Do you how it came into being?" I often find that many people have a Bible in their home, even nonbelievers and some atheists, so it is a topic for discussion. Seek to discover what others think and believe. If they are open or have questions, you could explain some of what we have discussed. It is also a lead-in to spiritual conversations. "Since we are talking about the Bible, do you know what the central message of the Bible is?" And then go to Romans 6:23 and the bridge illustration or whatever you are comfortable with.

Next Session (3 min.) Challenge members to bring articles. But realize that some will forget. You will want to have several articles and newspaper ads ready to hand out at this session, or at least have some ready next session for people who forget. We will focus on the reliability of the Scripture—its accuracy and truthfulness.

Close in Prayer (10 min.) Spend more time on personal issues because of the nature of the content at this meeting. Pray that we also would be "people of the book."

Session 3. Reliability & Truth: Why We Can Trust Our Bible.
Introduce the Session (3 min.) Go over the purpose and goal.

Purpose: This session will help us become fully confident in the accuracy and trustworthiness of the Word of God. To say that something is reliable and trustworthy means that it is without error and faithful in all it proclaims.

Goal: To give us the tools necessary to stand firm in our convictions that the Word of God is a reliable document and can stand up to the scrutiny of critics and serious students of the Scriptures.

Establishing Base Camp (10 min.) Ask members to get out the articles they brought with them. If they forgot, use yours. Give a brief overview of the article and determine whether the facts or information presented is truthful or not.

Then read the illustration and answer the question at the end about accuracy. Try to help your group understand that we regard so much written material as fact without ever testing the information. Discuss what some basic tests might be for determining the accuracy of something. Is it the author? What about witnesses? What if there were no witnesses, how can we believe? Try not to expose the tests of reliability outlined later in the study.

Ensure the group that we are not trying to attack Mormons. Most Mormons are moral people, good workers and good neighbors. Mormons are not the problem. But Mormon theology, history and writings do not stand up to the scrutiny of the Word of God or secular scholarship for that matter. A full treatment of Mormon teaching and the teachings of many other groups that deny the Bible or revise its teaching can be found in Walter Martin's book *Kingdom of the Cults.*

Mapping the Trail (10 min.) Allow members to express honest concerns here. Hopefully the study will increase their confidence in the Bible and give them a way to handle some of their issues. As they share, ask yourself these questions: Is this a matter of belief or understanding? Or is it about submission? Does someone truly not understand, or do they understand but the real problem is an unwillingness to accept it? Don't judge, but be discerning about people and their feelings and thoughts.

Comments may range from their ability to accept miracles, to why God judged Old Testament cultures or nations by allowing Israel to kill them in battle, to difficult prophecies or customs (particularly in the Old Testament). Respond simply by keeping the discussion going and acknowledging that some of the Bible is hard to understand. Give them hope and confidence that today's session will take them a few steps closer to believing the accuracy and truthfulness of the Bible. Let them also know that we cannot address all of the issues they might raise. (There are other studies in the Bible 101 series that can help address these.)

Beginning the Ascent (30 min.) Read through the information together, pausing to discuss questions that arise.

Reliability of the Bible. Cover the four tests here, and ask them to compare these tests to the guidelines they offered earlier in the meeting. We have only listed four major tests, and your group may come up with others that are also good.

One test should not be "Is the content believable?" In other words, some of the Bible is hard to believe. We have never seen anyone walk on water (unless it was frozen!). So the story of Jesus walking on water in Matthew 14, Mark 6 and John 6 would not be believable in and of itself. (If your neighbor said he walked on water while fishing last week, you would not believe him because he is not God.) But we know that he did walk on water because Jesus' life of miracles, attested to by hundreds and thousands of others who were truthful and reliable people, corroborated the evidence.

A fifth "test of reliability" may be added for believers in Christ, that is the testimony of the Holy Spirit. He works in us to confirm truth (see John 14:16-17, 26; 16:5-11; Romans 8:15-16). His teaching ministry in the believer helps us as we grow to discern the words of error from the words of truth. But this "test" cannot be used when looking at whether a document is reliable, the document and its authors must be evaluated as they are.

In discussing the question of why we must be so sure of the accuracy of the

Bible, guide the group toward the fact that our eternal destiny and standing before God is at stake. The claims of the Bible call us to change, repent, act, obey and love others in certain ways. If the Bible is not accurate, it has no right to make such claims on us (we will talk more of this in the next session on authority.)

You may want to spur on the discussion by mentioning these questions.

☐ Have you ever trusted someone only to have them break your trust? How long does it take to regain trust in a relationship?

☐ If God has lied to us, or if the writers have misrepresented him in some way, would we be able to trust him for our eternity?

☐ If the Bible cannot be trusted on matters of history and events, how can we place our trust in it for spiritual matters?

Gaining a Foothold (5 min.) Read this to your group. It reinforces what we just covered about the essential nature of the testimony of the Scriptures, and it demonstrates the absolute necessity of having reliable documents and trustworthy authors. Remember also that, based on 2 Peter 1:20-21, the Holy Spirit guided the writers (refer back to session one if necessary here).

Trailmarkers (10 min.) Read this and discuss it with the group. Often people assume that "spiritual" writers simply write their impressions about God. Much of what we see in the religion sections of today's bookstores is the mere opinions of men and women who claim to have had an experience with God or some spiritual force. There are no documents, no eyewitnesses, nothing to confirm. We must simply take the author's statements at face value. Thankfully this is not true of the Scriptures. If you have time before the meeting, you might visit a local bookstore and write down some of the titles of spiritual books and the claims made on the covers.

Teamwork (15 min.) Complete the exercise together and be sure to monitor the time. You want to have some time for discussion. Also, it might be fun to role-play the part of the friend. Have someone ask the presenter a few follow-up questions. This will provide a dialogue that is closer to real life. Look for people to use the information you discussed as part of their answer, but also look for their attitude. We are to present answers with gentleness and respect (1 Peter 3:15), not simply to prove we are right. Use good listening skills to first understand why your friend might have this question. What is at the heart of it?

Reaching the Summit (5 min.) Affirm members for "hanging in there" for some very technical material. Help them see this is not simply the kind of material that Bible scholars pay attention to, but that every believer must have a strong confidence in the Word and at least some data to back up their convictions.

Next Session (5 min.) Cover this with the group, asking them to prepare some thoughts for next time. What makes someone an authority? We will discuss why the Bible carries such authority and what our response needs to be.

Close in Prayer (10 min.) Spend time here affirming members, that they would grow in confidence in the Word. Spend time for other requests and needs as they arise.

Session 4. Authority: Why We Obey the Bible.
Introduce the Session (5 min.) Go over the purpose and goal.

Purpose: To get a firm understanding of the Bible's right to command belief and obedience, and to understand the nature of God's authority as primarily displayed in the words and works of Jesus.

Goal: To give us the perspective we need concerning God's authority and the impact it can have in our lives if we will yield ourselves to it.

Establishing Base Camp (10 min.) Read the personal illustration and the story of the centurion and discuss the questions that follow. The goal is to discover what constitutes authority. Sometimes it is someone's position, sometimes what they have accomplished, their age or their experience in a given subject area.

Mapping the Trail (10 min.) Try to get at the heart and attitude toward authority. Does anyone ever resent having a certain person over them in authority? How do people feel when they supervise someone who does not respect or acknowledge their authority? Here we are simply trying to get at feelings and perceptions of authority before looking at the Bible.

Beginning the Ascent (30 min.) Discuss the descriptions of authority and the questions listed. The reason we focus on Christ is because he is the central focus of all biblical history, claiming to be God in the flesh and calling men and women to make a decision about him. This would be grandiose or even arrogant if he were not God and his words were not true.

There are several passages listed here to support these five points. Do not read them all. Reference them for further study. If in your preparation you want to highlight a specific verse or two that's great. Focus on the questions and group interaction.

1. The Scripture speaks with authority. Help group members to understand that if the Bible is all we say it is (God's Word, truthful, powerful and so on), then we should read it more than twice a week, spending more time understanding what this great book calls us to do and be.

2. Jesus speaks with authority. A relationship with Jesus assumes obedience with his will. We cannot say we love him and not obey him. This is a powerful idea and people really need to let it sink in.

3. Jesus acts with authority. Brainstorm areas of life where our obedience is put to the test. Perhaps it is an area of temptation, an addictive behavior, a cut-throat work environment or an oppressive home life. Jesus may not always do miracles, but he does demonstrate that he is in control of these situations if we are willing to yield to his authority. It has been remarked that everything obeys Jesus—the wind, Satan, demons, disease—except for people!

4. Jesus' authority calls believers into action in his name. The scope of authority is the entire universe, and the source is God the Father. Jesus and the Father are both God. Jesus is fully human and fully divine, the God-man. But during his earthly ministry Jesus chose to become submissive to the Father and live out his humanity as an obedient servant to the Father and to the church. He did this to accomplish our redemption and to model the kind of life we are to live. (This is described in Philippians 2:5-11, which we will look at later in the session.) So at his return to the Father, his position of authority (which he willingly yielded) is restored by the Father and now he once again will reign as King of Kings. Even on earth he always possessed divine authority but chose to take the position of a servant. Now once again he has the position of authority, seated at the right hand of the Father (Hebrews 1:3). At the end of the age Jesus, the Lamb of God, will occupy the center place in eternal history to be worshiped by all (see Revelation 5; 7; 21).

5. Jesus' authority was observed by his followers. His miracles and words of power were seen firsthand by those who followed him. These are external claims to his authority, meaning they were given not by Jesus but by others who saw him.

Gaining a Foothold (5 min.) Read this to your group and then answer the questions. It is hard to obey Jesus because, frankly, we sometime don't believe he has our best interests in mind. This is a trust issue. Or a fear issue. We fear that obedience will cost us (and it will). We are not willing to pay the cost. We might lose friends, miss a promotion, incur loss of status or power or money. For example, someone might say, "I know I should not live with my boyfriend, but this is the first guy who has dated me in four years, and I am afraid he might leave, and no one will take his place." For some, obeying Jesus even puts them in harms way. Though this is not always the case, it makes many afraid to obey Jesus.

Trailmarkers (10 min.) Break into pairs and memorize John 14:23, or if this seems overwhelming for some people, give them John 14:15. It is interesting to note the comparison of these two verses. Jesus says in effect, "He who loves me, obeys me," and "He who obeys me, loves me." Discuss the relationship between love and obedience. Sometimes Jesus affirms that love leads to obedience (John 21:15-19), but in other settings, even when we don't feel like it, obedience is viewed by Christ as an expression of love (see also Matthew 21:28-32).

Allow the group a few minutes to discuss this relationship and their own walk with God related to love and obedience.

 Teamwork (15 min.) Complete the exercise together, spending five minutes on each section.

Today people can choose not to recognize Jesus' authority (Romans 1:21, 32); but one day everyone will submit to it, willingly or not (Philippians 2:10-11). Jesus has been in the role of Master and Servant. He knows what it takes and has willingly served (John 13) even though he had all the power of the divine ruler of the universe. Help the group reflect on this powerful irony. It is unique to Christianity that the one with the greatest power would be the servant of all, even allowing himself to be put to death by those he came to serve.

Push for personal application here. How is life affected by getting a firm grip on the authority of Jesus and the Bible?

Reaching the Summit (5 min.) Review the role of biblical authority and the need for our response to submit to Christ and his Word. We tend to rebel against authority, but God's authority has a purpose that actually benefits us. Take a moment to mention the benefits of a humble, obedient life with Christ. Then read aloud 1 John 5:3 and 2 John 5:6 to the group.

Next Session (5 min.) Challenge people to memorize the books of the Bible. This is not just busywork. It will give them a grasp on where to find things and also set them up for a discussion of why the Bible books were chosen. The Bible 101 study entitled *Cover to Cover* deals with the various sections of the Bible.

Close in Prayer (10 min.) Spend time affirming members, praying for each other to be growing in submission to God, obedience to his Word and eagerness to do his will. Pray for needs in the group.

Session 5. Canon: What Books Were Included & Why.

Introduce the Session (5 min.) Go over the purpose and goal.

Purpose: To understand how the sixty-six books of the Bible came to be in the Christian canon.

Goal: To gain confidence that these books—and only these sixty-six books—constitute Scripture, and to understand the process by which they were recognized as such by the early church.

Establishing Base Camp (10 min.) This story is from the *Gospel of Thomas*. This particular reading was translated by Montague Rhodes James (Oxford, 1924) in *The Apocryphal New Testament*.

Read the story and the questions. The point here is to have some fun, and ask people if they ever read this in the Bible. You might even playfully tell them that it is one of your favorites because there are so few stories about Jesus' life as a child. Basically, we are setting the stage for how we know that something is Scripture. Some people still wonder if we have all the books, and why Roman Catholic Bibles have books that Protestant Bibles do not.

Mapping the Trail (10 min.) Later we will look at the tests of canonicity—what is it that provides the standard for the canon of Scripture. Here we want to see what guidelines your group can come up with.

Beginning the Ascent (30 min.) Review the definition of *canon* with your group. You might ask: What standards or guidelines must be met in your work? Or what standard do you have for your kids? What role do standards play in our lives? Measures of authenticity are used today for antique furniture, artwork and other collectibles. Title searches for real estate are common, again to ensure that "this is the correct property." So the idea of a canon is not so far-fetched. Then go over the section entitled "Why Bother with a Canon?" Finally, go over the material under "Tests of the Canon," referring back to "Mapping the Trail" and comparing the tests you discussed with the three tests described in the session.

1. Doctrinal soundness. Did the writing square up with the teachings of Christ, the teachings of other apostles and the teachings of the Old Testament Scriptures? If not, it was not considered Scripture. Here we are basically asking, Does it have the feel of true Scripture? The early Jewish Rabbis said the Scripture "soiled the hands," meaning that it was so pure that even holding the word of God made you feel dirty.

2. Recognition by the church. Again emphasize that the church merely affirmed what everyone already believed. This was an official process to make a public, church-wide statement in the midst of false teaching and the circulation of suspect documents.

Gaining a Foothold (10 min.) Do not get into a debate here about the Catholic Bible and Apocrypha versus Protestant versions of the Scripture. Scholars have never accepted the Apocrypha, but late church councils and the Vatican gave credence to these writings. The point here is to show that there were other spiritual writings competing for space in the Bible, but the church rejected them outright with little debate because the writings were always found to have inaccuracies and doctrinal errors.

Trailmarkers (10 min.) When Paul says "all Scripture," technically he would have only had an Old Testament scroll as his Bible. But he is writing late in his life and had already written much of the New Testament. So it is likely that in his mind he may have been including the inspired writings of his own or others he was aware of. In any case, memorize this important verse because it focuses on the ultimate reasons for the Word of God, a changed life.

Teamwork (15 min.) Read and discuss the passages, noting the following:
1 Timothy 5:18: Quoting Deuteronomy 25:4 and Luke 10:7 implies that Paul considered New Testament writings like Luke's as authoritative Scripture. This would be dropping a huge bombshell to the average Jew who did not follow Christ.

How could anyone call Luke's work "Scripture"? But Paul did!

1 Thessalonians 2:13: The Word of God is the apostolic preaching delivered mainly by him. If his preaching is considered the Word of God, then Paul is stating that his teaching (and by implication, his writing) is the Word of God.

2 Peter 3:15-16: Peter puts Paul's writings in the same category as "other Scriptures."

Revelation 22:18-19: John was probably not referring to all of the Bible. He was in exile on the island of Patmos, and it is unlikely that he had a full copy, especially since books of the New Testament were just beginning to be put together in groups, mostly collections of letters or the four Gospels bound together. But he certainly says that Revelation is the culmination of the biblical writings. Jude 3-4 also gives us evidence that there was not much left to talk about because the faith had been "delivered" and now we are to protect it. Verses like this give support, along with the death of the apostles, that the canon was closed after Revelation.

▲ **Reaching the Summit (5 min.)** Remind people that they have tackled some material usually reserved only for those in seminaries. Explain to them that they can understand this and gain confidence in the Bible. Perhaps a brief review of how far they have come in five sessions is in order. Celebrate your progress and allow for a final question or two.

Here's a brief summary of each session.

Session one: The Bible is God's specific revelation to us, coauthored by the Holy Spirit (who protected it from error) and the writers. It's source is God, and the product is an error-free text.

Session two: The manuscripts of the Bible are many and provide evidence for an accurate text today. Using a variety of translation methods (literal, dynamic equivalent, paraphrase), translators have given us many versions of the Bible to use for study and evaluation.

Session three: The Bible is absolutely reliable in all it teaches. All evidence points to a trustworthy text which passes the tests of character, corroboration, conviction and consistency.

Session four: Because the Bible comes from God and is truthful, it is authoritative and requires our response. Central to its authority is the authority of Jesus Christ over all things and all people.

Session five: The canon of Scripture—sixty-six books—is the final and complete written Word of God. The books were inherently authoritative, doctrinally sound, attested to by the apostles and prophets, and affirmed by the early church.

Next Session (5 min.) Bring your Bible and your study guide to the next session. Come prepared to tackle a project together. Encourage them not to read ahead to the next session. It is a project designed to be done *in* the meeting.

Close in Prayer (10 min.) Pray for needs in the group.

Session 6. Putting It All Together.

Introduce the Session (5 min.) Go over the purpose and goal.

Purpose: To use what the group has discovered over the last five sessions and apply it to a real life situation.

Goal: To craft an accurate and confident response to someone challenging the reliability and authority of the Bible.

Establishing Base Camp (10 min.) Take a few minutes to review in very broad ways what has been covered in the last five sessions. This is an overview, not a detailed summary. You might even have some fun and ask a few people what inspiration is, or encourage them to recall the tests of the canon, or what is meant by "the authority of the Bible." Put them at ease for the night and ask them to enjoy the adventure.

Teamwork (45 min.) It is not unusual in our culture to pick up a magazine, a book or a newspaper and find someone questioning the Bible. Even though we have covered some data that does not "sizzle" like the stories of the New Testament, it is information that affects how people view and understand the Bible. And when a respected pastor casts doubt on the reliability of the Word of God, people can get pretty confused.

Your role in this session is to help people integrate all they have learned, to pull it together and apply it with confidence. Keep the discussion moving, and break into smaller groups if you think that would be best. Stay with the focus of the lesson and do not get into discussions about some of the doctrinal issues raised by Pastor Dave. We simply do not have the time to deal with everything in detail.

Refer to the four questions in the participant's section. You may want to assign questions to teams or try to do it as a group. It depends on the size of the group and the time you have. Make sure there is about fifteen minutes at the end for discussion. Here is some information to help you guide or clarify the discussion.

1. Here you want the group to come to the conclusion that God's Word is accurate and reliable because (a) he spoke it through special revelation to us; and (b) the Holy Spirit guided the process and worked with the writers, keeping error from the manuscripts (the dual authorship of Scripture). Pastor Dave thinks that we hold to the "dictation view" of inspiration. But we do not. Notice how the rest of his argument is really based on this first point. Once you allow for errors, anything and everything in the Bible is up for grabs!

2. If God does not communicate with words, how do we know he exists? Granted, some of his communication takes place that way, but only to give us a general impression that he exists and is greater than we are (Psalm 19; Romans 1:18-23.) But the message of salvation, instructions for the church, guidelines for moral behavior and help for wise decision-making must all be communicated in words!

3. How would Dave know that God is loving and kind? The Bible! If he relies on the Bible to tell him about God's love, why not his judgment and dealing with

evil and sin? He has a "good God—bad God" view of the God of the Bible. We can only trust the "good God" statements. The "good God" is the real God, the "bad God" is invented by the writers of the Bible.

He has a low view of the authority of the Bible. It is only an authority when it teaches what he agrees with or how he perceives God. This process of studying the Bible uses what is called *eisegesis* (pronounced ice-eh-gee-sis), which means "reading into the text," instead of *exegesis* (ex-eh-gee-sis), which means "drawing out of the text." If we read into it anything we want, we become the authority. But if the text is the Word of God, brimming with authority, then we are do draw out of it what it says, not what we want it to say. Most people simply do not want to let God have authority over them.

Also be aware that Dave is using a metaphorical approach to interpretation, not taking things at face value but assigning a deeper more mystical meaning to the story. If he takes Jonah at face value, he finds the story absurd. So the story could not possibly be true. It's just a story made up to make a point. It does not matter if there was a real Jonah or a whale or a city of Nineveh. This, in his opinion, is a story on the same level as C. S. Lewis' *Chronicles of Narnia* or Mark Twain's *Tom Sawyer*.

4. When Jonah is relegated to fairy tale status, then it is no longer Scripture. If it is a fairy tale it cannot command belief, speak for God or be used by the Holy Spirit in his teaching ministry. None of the early Jewish leaders or early church leaders rejected the historicity of Jonah. They recognized it as canonical. It has only been liberal scholars of the nineteenth and twentieth centuries who have argued that the book could not be true. These same people reject the miracles of Jesus, his physical resurrection and his virgin birth (not much left of Christianity after that!).

Look at Matthew 12:39-42. Jesus speaks of the book of Jonah as historical and even links the story of his death and resurrection to it (12:40). If, as Pastor Dave would argue, Jonah was not actually in the fish (not a whale, as Dave assumes) for three days, then Jesus prediction of his death and resurrection are based on a fairy tale. Second, Jesus says that the repentant people of Nineveh, who responded to Jonah's preaching, will judge the current generation for their unbelief. If Jonah is a fable, then the threat of judgment given by Jesus against the hardhearted and evil Pharisees in this passage is meaningless! What made the Pharisees' blood curdle was that the transformation at Nineveh was authentic.

Reaching the Summit (5 min.) Celebrate the end of this study and affirm each group member in front of the others by recognizing their efforts and hard work.

Next Session (5 min.) Determine a time and place to celebrate if this is your last meeting together. If not, decide on your next study and move ahead!

Close in Prayer (10 min.) Focus your prayers on group needs and on thanksgiving for all God has taught us during these sessions together.